John F. Kennedy

by Helen Frost

Consulting Editor: Gail Saunders-Smith, Ph.D.

Consultant: James N. Druckman, Ph.D.,
Assistant Professor of Political Science,
University of Minnesota

Pebble Books

an imprint of Capstone Press
Mankato, Minnesota

Pebble Books are published by Capstone Press
151 Good Counsel Drive, P.O. Box 669, Mankato, Minnesota 56002
http://www.capstone-press.com

1 2 3 4 5 6 08 07 06 05 04 03

Library of Congress Cataloging-in-Publication Data
Frost, Helen, 1949–
John F. Kennedy / by Helen Frost
   p. cm.—(Famous Americans)
   Summary: An introduction to the life of the thirty-fifth president of the United
States.
   Includes bibliographical references and index.
   ISBN 0-7368-1642-9 (hardcover)
   1. Kennedy, John F. (John Fitzgerald), 1917–1963—Juvenile literature.
2. Presidents—United States—Biography—Juvenile literature. [1. Kennedy, John F.
(John Fitzgerald), 1917–1963. 2. Presidents.] I. Title. II. Series.
E842.Z9 F765 2003
973.922′092—dc21   2002011743

Note to Parents and Teachers

The Famous Americans series supports national history standards for units on people and culture. This book describes and illustrates the life of John F. Kennedy. The photographs support early readers in understanding the text. This book also introduces early readers to subject-specific vocabulary words, which are defined in the Words to Know section. Early readers may need assistance in reading some words and to use the Table of Contents, Words to Know, Read More, Internet Sites, and Index/Word List sections of the book.

Table of Contents

John F. Kennedy was born in Massachusetts on May 29, 1917. He had eight brothers and sisters. John liked to spend time with his family.

John pictured with his parents and seven of his siblings

John wanted to study history and politics. He went to Harvard University.

8

John joined the navy in 1941. He was the lieutenant of a boat. The boat sank. John helped the crew swim to safety.

John wanted to help people.
He became a politician.
John was elected to the
House of Representatives.
Later, he was elected to
the Senate.

John married Jacqueline
Bouvier in 1953. They had
three children. The children
were named Caroline,
John Jr., and Patrick.
Patrick lived for only
two days.

14

John was elected president of the United States in 1960. He was 43 years old. He was the youngest person to be elected president.

As president, John worked with many world leaders. He worked for peace. John started the Peace Corps.

John thought all people should be treated fairly.
He worked for equal rights.

On November 22, 1963, John was shot during a parade in Dallas, Texas. He died. We remember John F. Kennedy as a great leader of our nation.

Words to Know

elect—to choose someone or decide something by voting

history—the study of past events

House of Representatives—one of the two groups of the U.S. Congress that makes laws; members are elected to two-year terms.

Peace Corps—an organization of trained volunteers from the United States that helps people in other countries with jobs such as farming and teaching

politician—someone who runs for or holds a government office

politics—the activity involved in governing a country

Senate—one of the two groups of the U.S. Congress that makes laws; members are elected to six-year terms.

Read More

Harper, Judith E. *John F. Kennedy: Our Thirty-Fifth President.* Our Presidents. Chanhassen, Minn.: Child's World, 2002.

Joseph, Paul. *John F. Kennedy.* United States Presidents. Minneapolis: Abdo and Daughters, 2000.

Raatma, Lucia. *John F. Kennedy.* Profiles of the Presidents. Minneapolis: Compass Point Books, 2002.

Internet Sites

Track down many sites about John F. Kennedy. Visit the FACT HOUND at *http://www.facthound.com*

IT IS EASY! IT IS FUN!

1) Go to *http://www.facthound.com*

2) Type in: 0736816429

3) Click on "FETCH IT" and FACT HOUND will find several links hand-picked by our editors.

Relax and let our pal FACT HOUND do the research for you!

23

Index/Word List

boat, 9
born, 5
Bouvier,
   Jacqueline, 13
brothers, 5
Caroline, 13
children, 13
Dallas, 21
died, 21
elected, 11, 15
equal rights, 19
family, 5
Harvard
   University, 7

history, 7
House of
   Representatives,
   11
John Jr., 13
leader, 17, 21
lieutenant, 9
married, 13
Massachusetts, 5
nation, 21
navy, 9
Patrick, 13
Peace Corps, 17
politician, 11

politics, 7
president, 15, 17
Senate, 11
shot, 21
sisters, 5
swim, 9
Texas, 21
United States, 15
world, 17
youngest, 15

Word Count: 190
Early-Intervention Level: 18

Editorial Credits
Hollie J. Endres, editor; Molly Nei, designer; Clay Schotzko/Icon Productions,
   cover designer; Karrey Tweten, photo researcher

Photo Credits
Getty Images/Hulton Archive, 1, 6, 12, 16, 20; Fabian Bachrach, cover;
   Frank Turgent, 8
The John F. Kennedy Library, 4, 10, 18
NASA, 14

The author thanks the children's library staff at the Allen County Public Library in
Fort Wayne, Indiana, for research assistance.